SMILE-A-WHILE

SPORTS JOKES

By Gary Chmielewski
Drawings by Ron G. Clark

Library of Congress Cataloging in Publication Data

Chmielewski, Gary, 1946-
  Sports.

  (Smile-a-while joke book)
  Summary: A collection of jokes and riddles about sports, such as "What do a bat and a fly swatter have in common? They both hit flies."
    1. Sports—Juvenile humor.   2. Wit and humor, Juvenile.   [1. Sports—Wit and humor.   2. Jokes.
3. Riddles]   I. Title.   II. Series.
PN6231.S65C4   1986   818'.5402   86-17772
ISBN 0-86592-683-2

ROURKE ENTERPRISES, INC.
VERO BEACH, FLORIDA 32964

When is a boxer like an astronomer?
When he sees stars!

George: What's the score of the game?
Belinda: 21 to 13
George: Who's winning?
Belinda: 21

Why would a spider make a good outfielder?
He's good at catching flies!

Arnie: I always carry a spare pair of pants with me when I golf.
Sammy: Why?
Arnie: I might get a hole-in-one.

What three "R's" do cheerleaders have to learn?
Rah! Rah! Rah!

What two things can't a runner have for breakfast?
Lunch and dinner!

Rookie: How do you hold a bat?
Veteran: By its wings.

Why is bowling such a quiet game?
You can hear a pin drop!

Where do judges go to relax?
The tennis court!

Why is the stadium the coolest place?
All the fans are in the stands.

Why did the basketball player bring a shotgun to the game?
He wanted to shoot the ball!

Reporter: Have you ever hunted bear?
Sportsman: No, but I've gone fishing in my bathing suit!

Did you hear about the person who went to the football game because he thought the quarterback was a refund?

What kind of sand would you run in if you wanted to be faster?
Quicksand!

Does horseback riding give you a headache?
No, quite the reverse!

Paul: Doctor, will I be able to play soccer after my leg heals?
Doctor: Of course.
Paul: Great. I never could play before.

What monster goes to baseball games?
A double-header!

Henry: Did you hear the new song about baseball?
Babe: No, why?
Henry: You should, it's a really big hit!

Julie: I don't play tennis anymore because it's too noisy.
Debbie: Too noisy?
Julie: Yeah, everyone raises a racket.

Why is a basketball player's hand never larger than eleven inches?
If it were twelve inches, it would be a foot!

Which professional football team has the largest players?
The New York GIANTS!

To what football game do you have to bring crackers and a spoon?
The Soup-er Bowl! (Yeah — Chicago Bears)

Rookie: What does it take to hit a ball the way you do?
Veteran: A bat.

Little Girl: What kind of fish is that?
Fisherman: Smelt.
Little Girl: It sure does. But what kind of fish is it?

Umpire: I have to admit, the players on your team are good losers.
Coach: Good? They're perfect!

Christy: We can't go swimming right now. After eating, mom said we shouldn't swim on a full stomach.

Laura: Okay – we'll swim on our backs.

Game Warden: Kids, you can't fish without a permit!

Jimmy: Not so, sir. We're using worms and the fish are biting like crazy!

Basketball fan: I bet I can tell you the score of this game before it starts.

Sportcaster: Okay, smartie, tell me.

Basketball fan: Nothing to nothing.

What has 18 legs and catches flies?
A baseball team.

Why should everyone run?
We all belong to the human race!

In what part of the car do you keep your baseball mitt?
The glove compartment!

Why is it so hard to drive a golf ball?
No steering wheel!

Did you hear about the college athlete who won a letter in football and asked a friend to read it to him?

First Hunter: This must be a good place for hunting.
Second Hunter: How do yo know?
First Hunter: The sign said "Fine For Hunting!"

Charles: I went riding today.
Diana: Horseback?
Charles: Sure – about two hours before me.

Gary: My father went hunting today and shot three turkeys.
Laura: Were they wild?
Gary: No, but the farmer who owned them sure was.

Baseball Manager to Outfielders: You've been missing a lot of balls out there lately. If you can't do any better, I'm going to have to put in some other players.
Outfielders: Gee thanks! We can use the help!

What do eggs and a losing ball team have in common?
They both get beaten.

Jean: I've been skiing since I was five years old.
Ron: You must really be tired!

Who won at Bull Run?
I don't know — was the score in the papers?

What's a mosquito's favorite sport?
Skin diving!

How do you kiss a hockey player?
You pucker up!

Why was the baseball player arrested after the season?
He stole 85 bases.

Gary: Why don't you play golf with Terry anymore?

Jimmy: Would you play with a cheat who moves the ball when you're not looking and writes down the wrong score?

Gary: Certainly not!

Jimmy: Well, neither will Terry!

Why are waiters and waitresses such good tennis players?
They know how to serve!

Which football player wears the biggest shoes?
The one with the biggest feet.

Why is basketball such a sloppy sport?
All the players dribble!

Why is an airline pilot like a running back?
They both want to make a touchdown!

Old Fisherman: Did you ever take home a fish this size, sonny?
Sonny: No, sir. I always throw the little ones back.

Why does it take longer to run from second base to third than it does from first to second base?
There's a shortstop between second and third.

Game Warden: Do you know that you are hunting with last year's license?
Hunter: It's Okay – I'm only after the ones that got away last year!

What do a bat and a fly swatter have in common?
They both hit flies.

Game Warden: Young man, there's no fishing here!
Young Man: You're telling me! I've been here for two hours and haven't had a bite.

Charlie: Mom, I'm going out to play soccer.
Mom: With your new slacks?
Charlie: No, with the boys down the street!

Why couldn't the fans drink soda during the second baseball game?
The home team lost the opener.

What happens to old bowling balls?
They become marbles for elephants.

Gail: I'm taking a course in parachute jumping.
Tommy: How many jumps do you have to make before you pass the course?
Gail: All of them!

What has three feet and no legs?
A yardstick.

What was the chicken farmer doing at the basketball game?
Looking for fouls (fowls)!

Which winter sport do you learn in the fall?
Ice skating!

What's the biggest jewel in the world?
A baseball diamond.